Alphabet Letter Tracing For Preschoolers

Information for Parents

The development of fine motor skills, like writing, aids in improving reading speed and accuracy for young children.

As your child progresses from using larger items like crayons, large pencils, or marker pens, the development of writing becomes an important developmental skill for all children.

This book will help your child to:
- Gain exposure to letters from the alphabet.
- Become aware of the shapes and structures of each letter and number.
- Develop writing muscle memory with the development of fine motor skill developed through repetition.
- Assist children in getting to know the alphabet and learn basic word structures.

This book has been designed in progressive stages so the child can build confidence throughout each section. The child will initially focus on straight lines and shapes with tracing patterns and interactive activities then progress to letters and shapes beginning with capital letters and then lower case letters.

We are excited to help your child on their educational journey as they learn to write, and we hope your child has fun along the journey by using this book.

LETTER

Ant

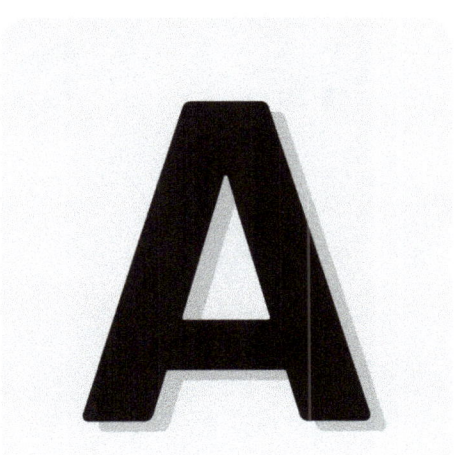

A A A A A A A

A A A A A A A

A A A A A A A

A A A A A A A

A A A A A A A

Try the letters yourself in the space below

LETTER

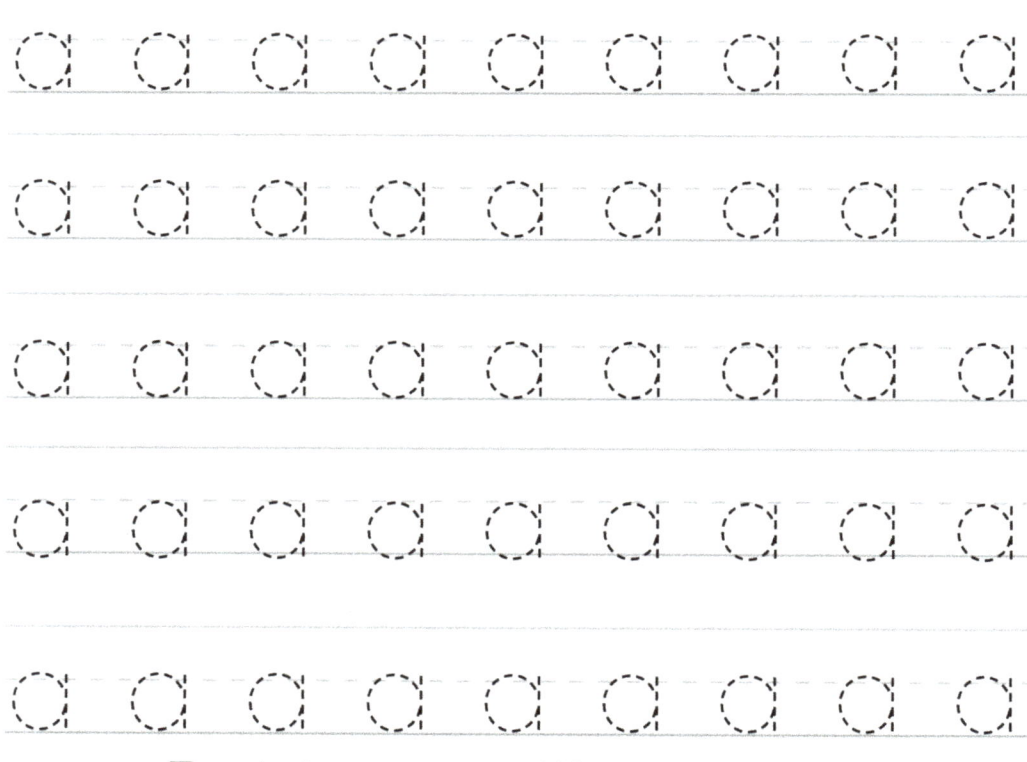

Try the letters yourself in the space below

LETTER

Bee

B B B B B B B B
B B B B B B B B
B B B B B B B B
B B B B B B B B
B B B B B B B B

Try the letters yourself in the space below

LETTER

bear

b b b b b b b b b
b b b b b b b b b
b b b b b b b b b
b b b b b b b b b
b b b b b b b b b

Try the letters yourself in the space below

LETTER

 clock

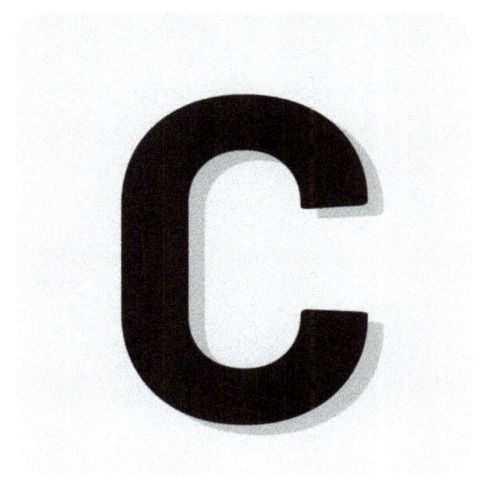

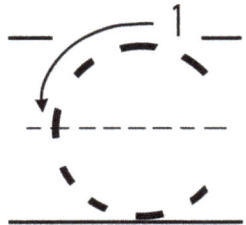

Try the letters yourself in the space below

LETTER C

cat

Try the letters yourself in the space below

LETTER

Dog

Try the letters yourself in the space below

LETTER

 drum

Try the letters yourself in the space below

LETTER

Elephant

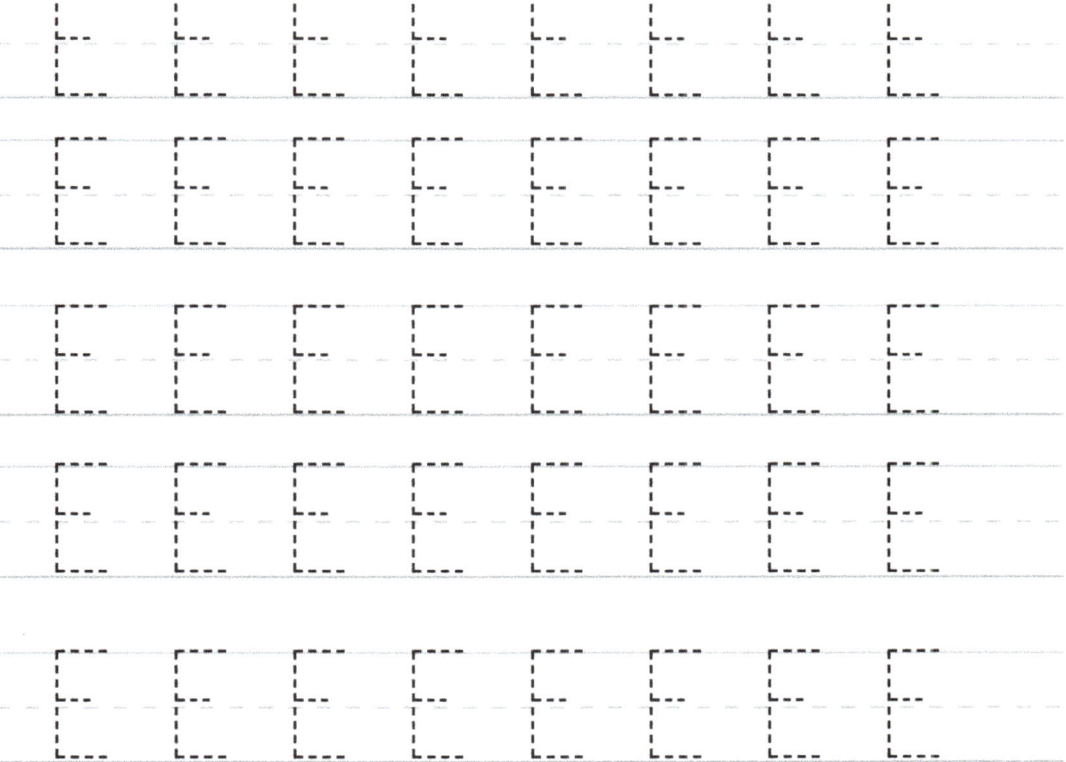

Try the letters yourself in the space below

LETTER

 **e**gg

Try the letters yourself in the space below

LETTER

 F|y

Try the letters yourself in the space below

LETTER

 **f**rog

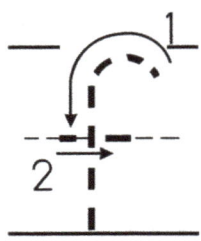

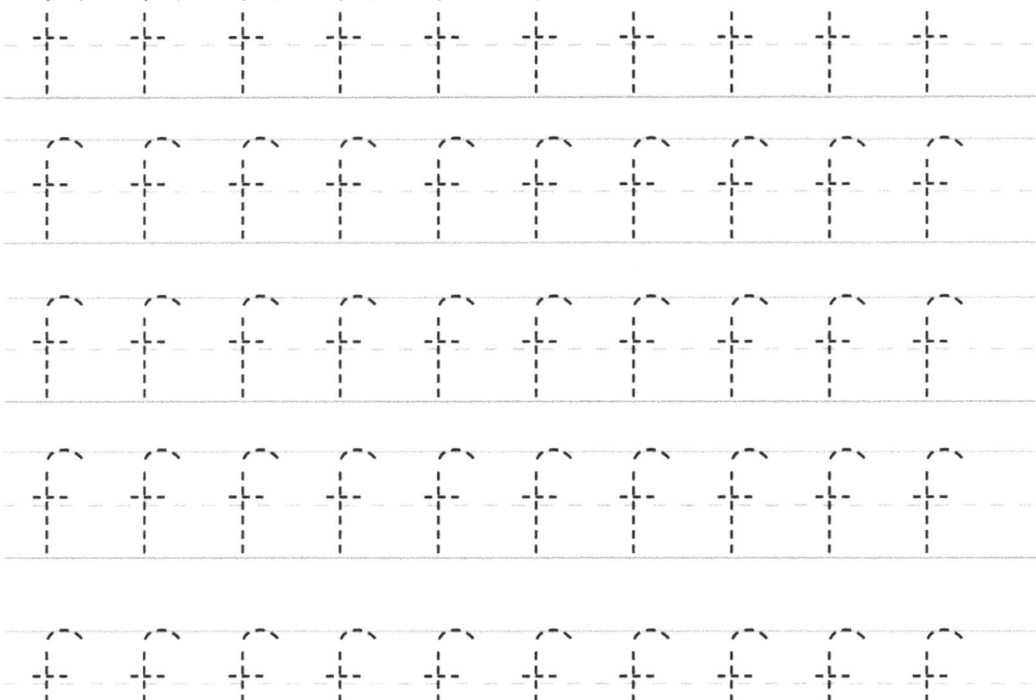

Try the letters yourself in the space below

LETTER

 **G**oat

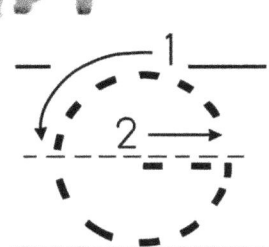

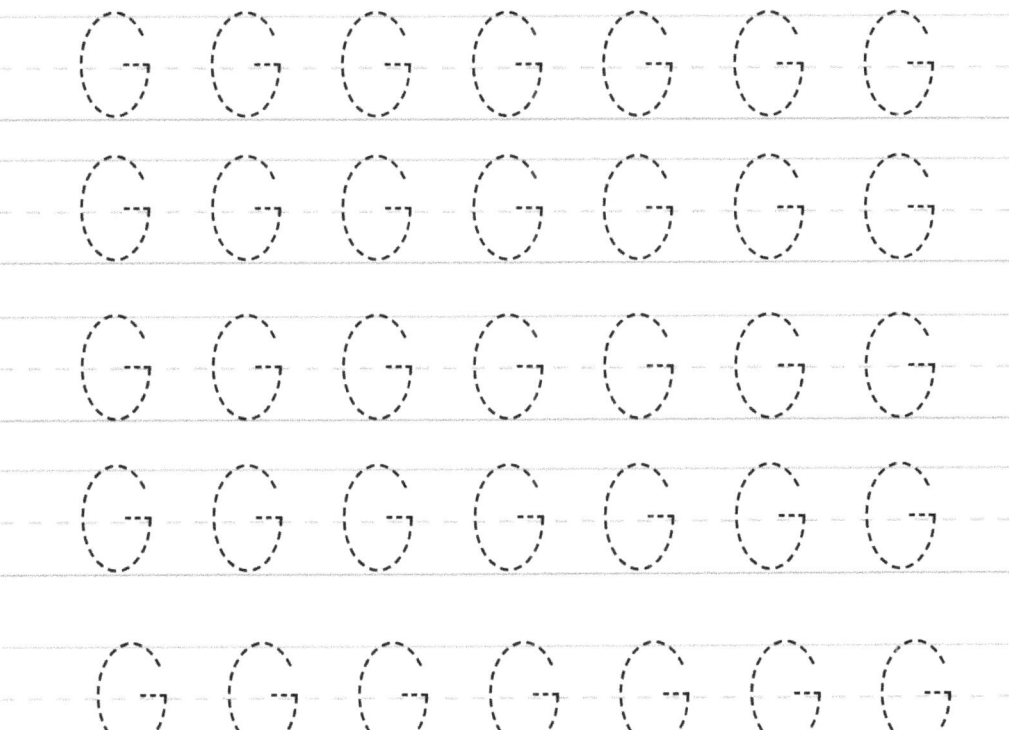

Try the letters yourself in the space below

LETTER

Try the letters yourself in the space below

LETTER H

Helicopter

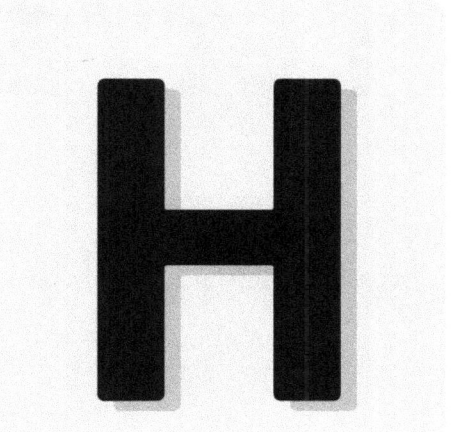

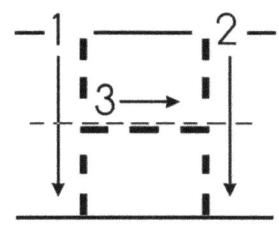

Try the letters yourself in the space below

LETTER

hat

Try the letters yourself in the space below

LETTER

Igloo

Try the letters yourself in the space below

LETTER

  **i**nsect

Try the letters yourself in the space below

LETTER J

Jaguar

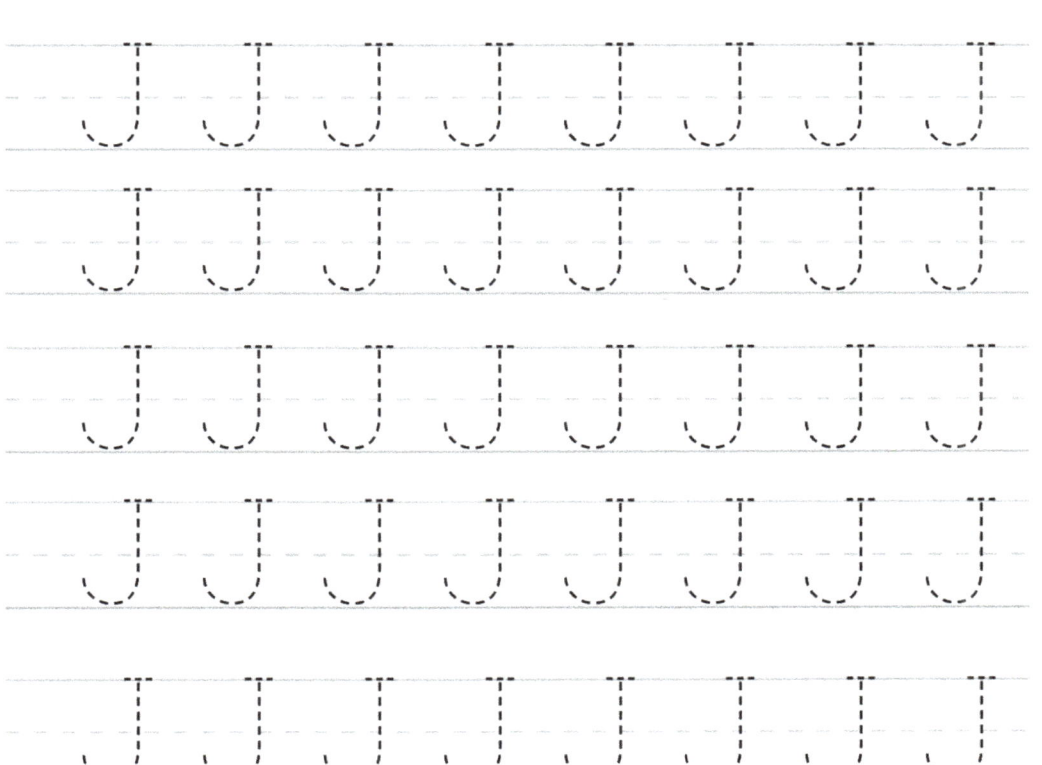

Try the letters yourself in the space below

LETTER

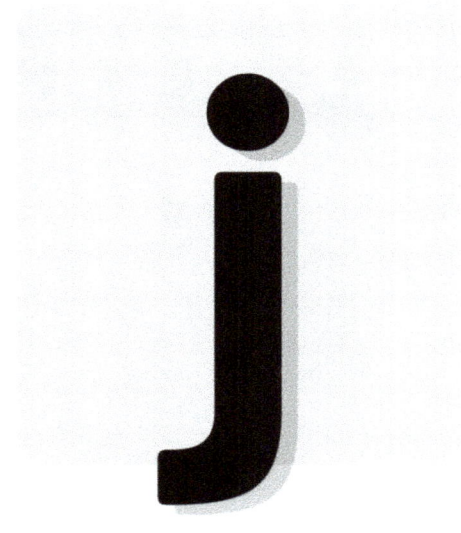

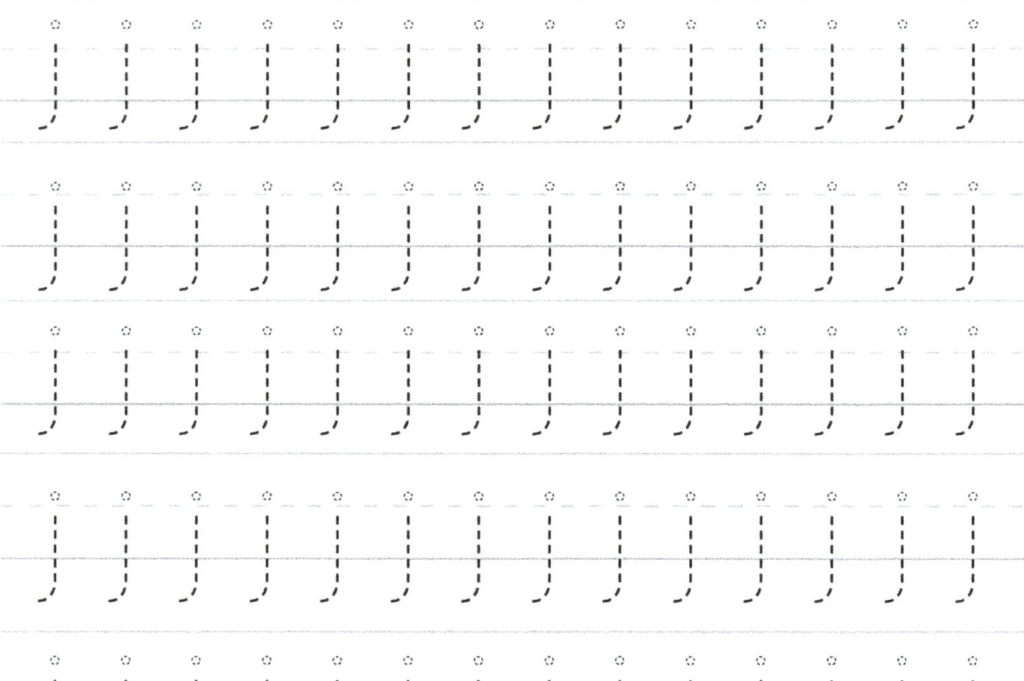

Try the letters yourself in the space below

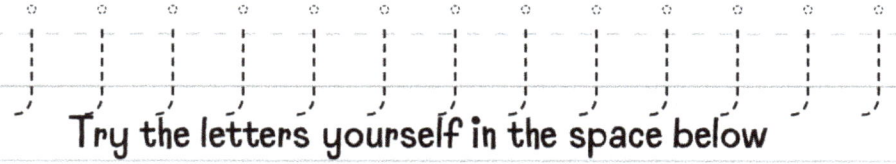

LETTER

koala

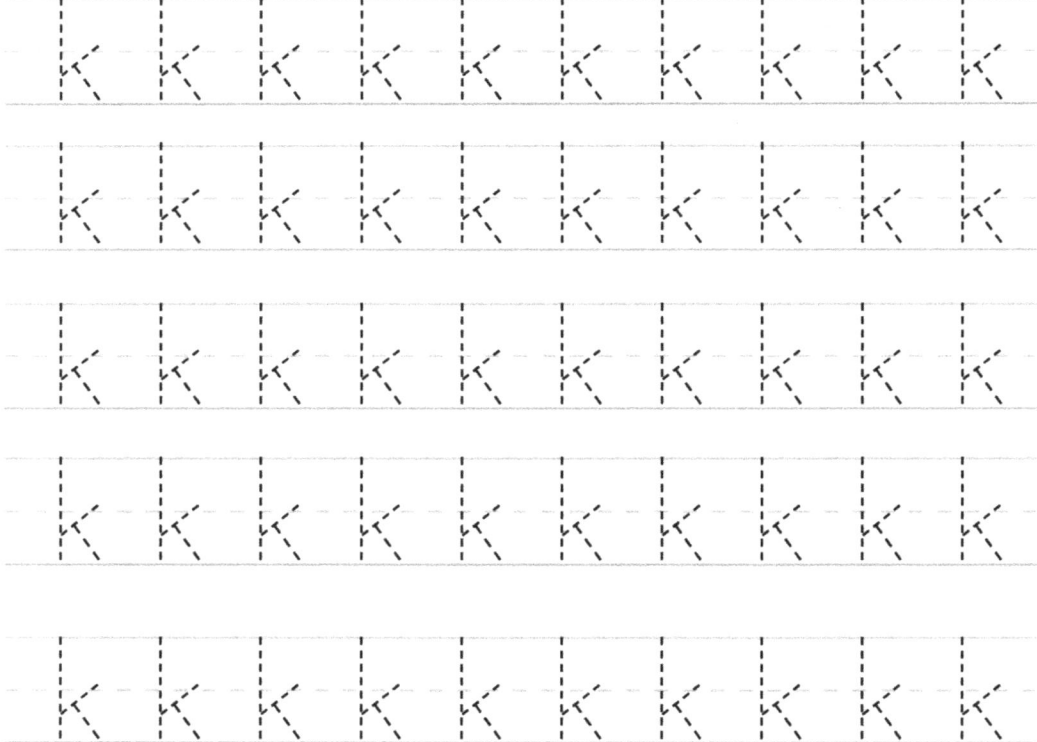

Try the letters yourself in the space below

LETTER

 Lemon

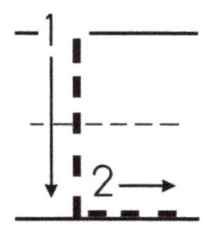

L L L L L L L L L
L L L L L L L L L
L L L L L L L L L
L L L L L L L L L
L L L L L L L L L

Try the letters yourself in the space below

LETTER
lizard

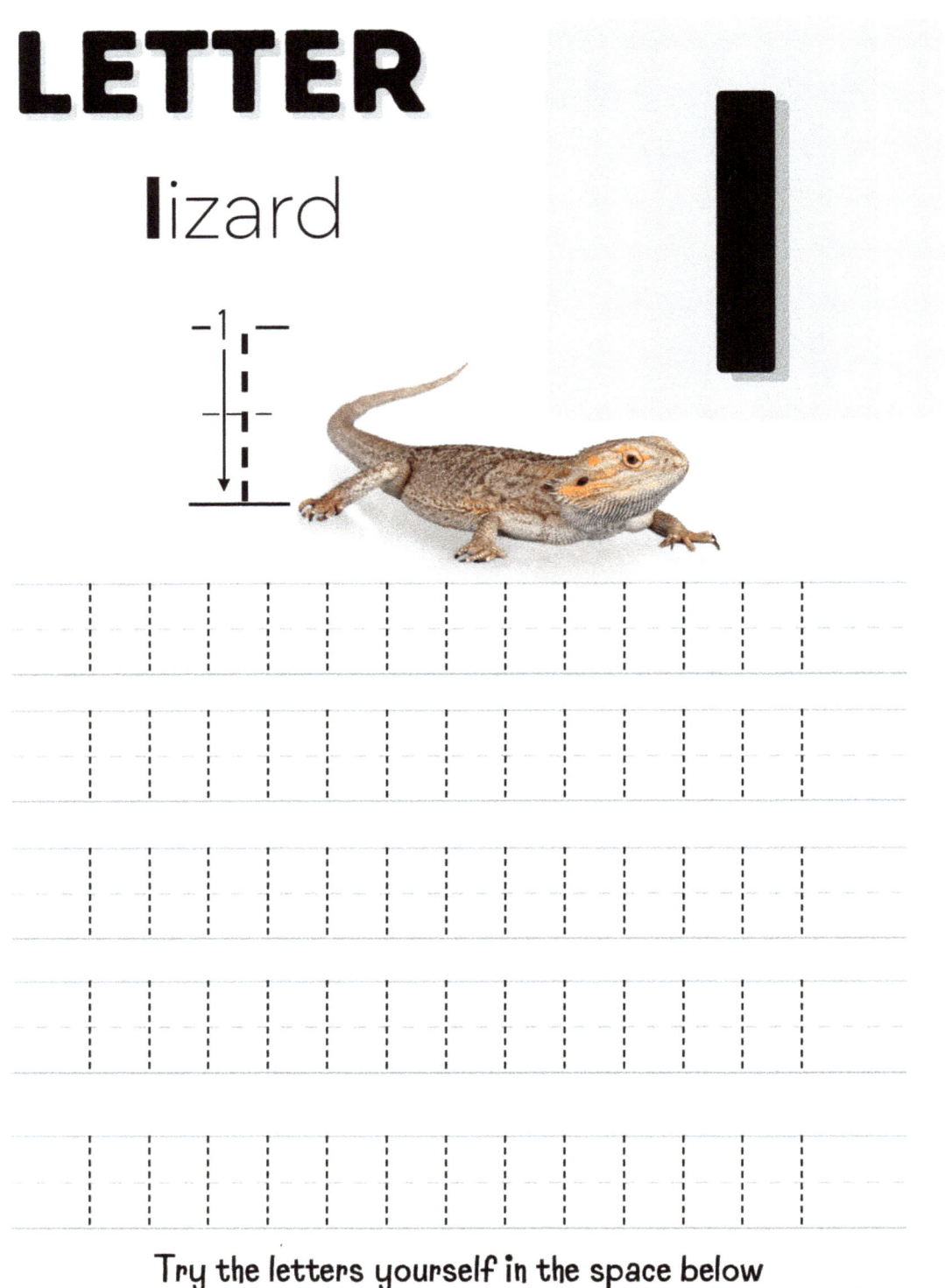

Try the letters yourself in the space below

LETTER

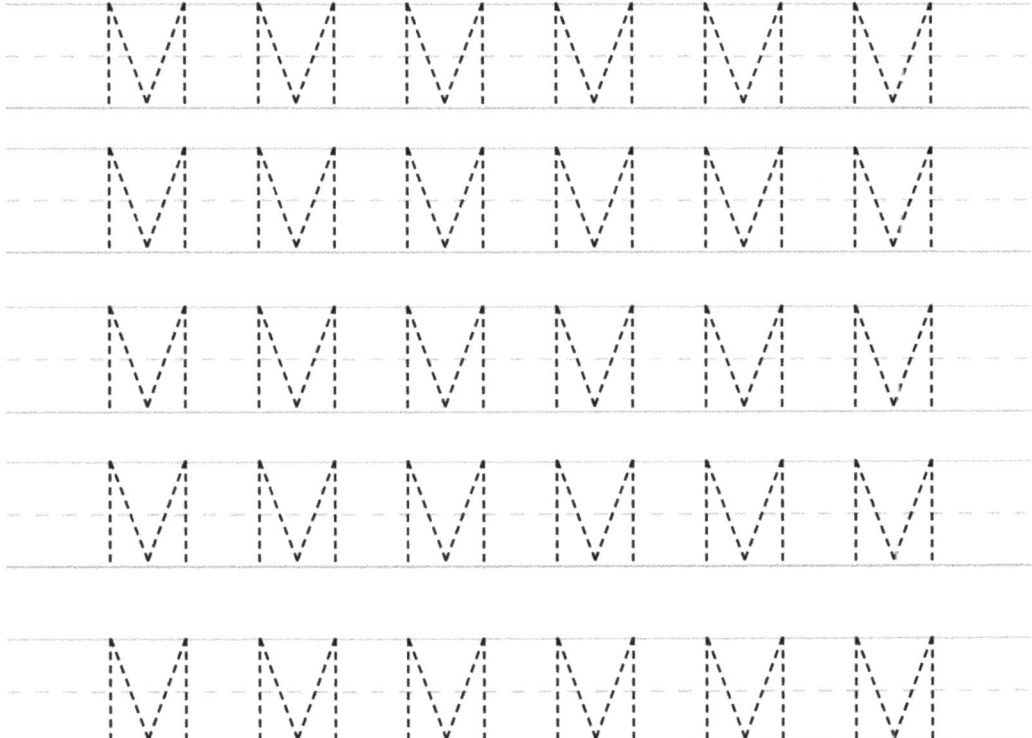

Try the letters yourself in the space below

LETTER

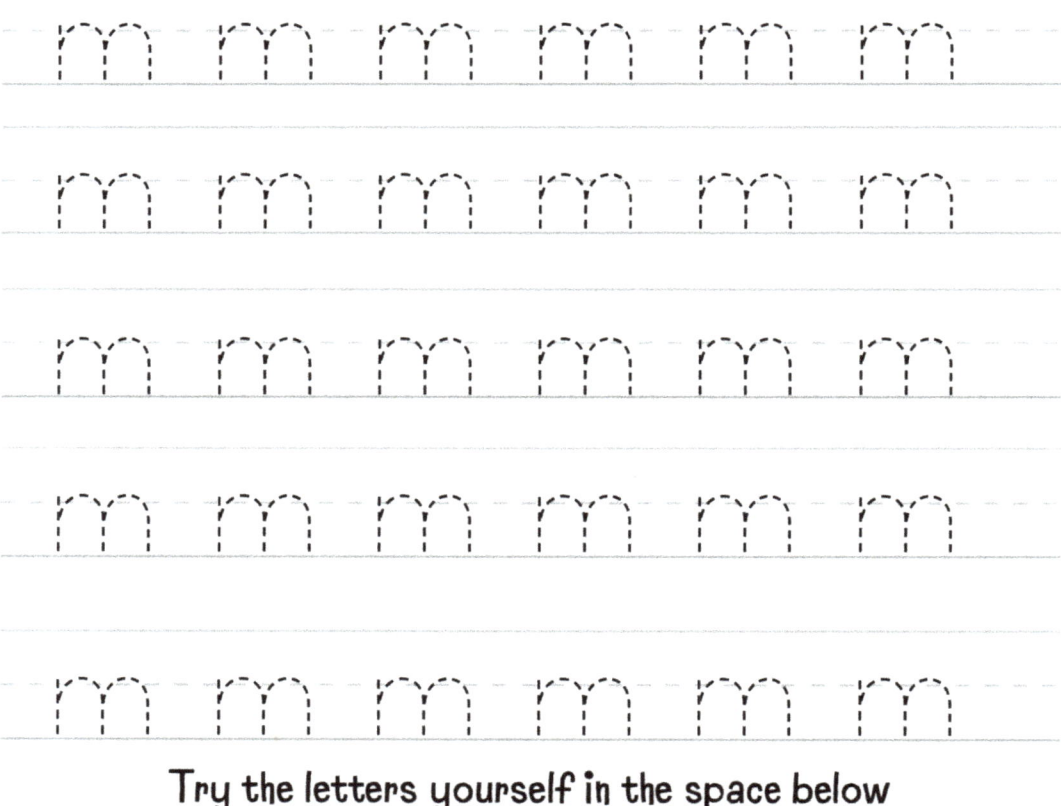

Try the letters yourself in the space below

LETTER N

Nest

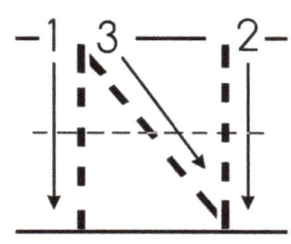

Try the letters yourself in the space below

LETTER

nail

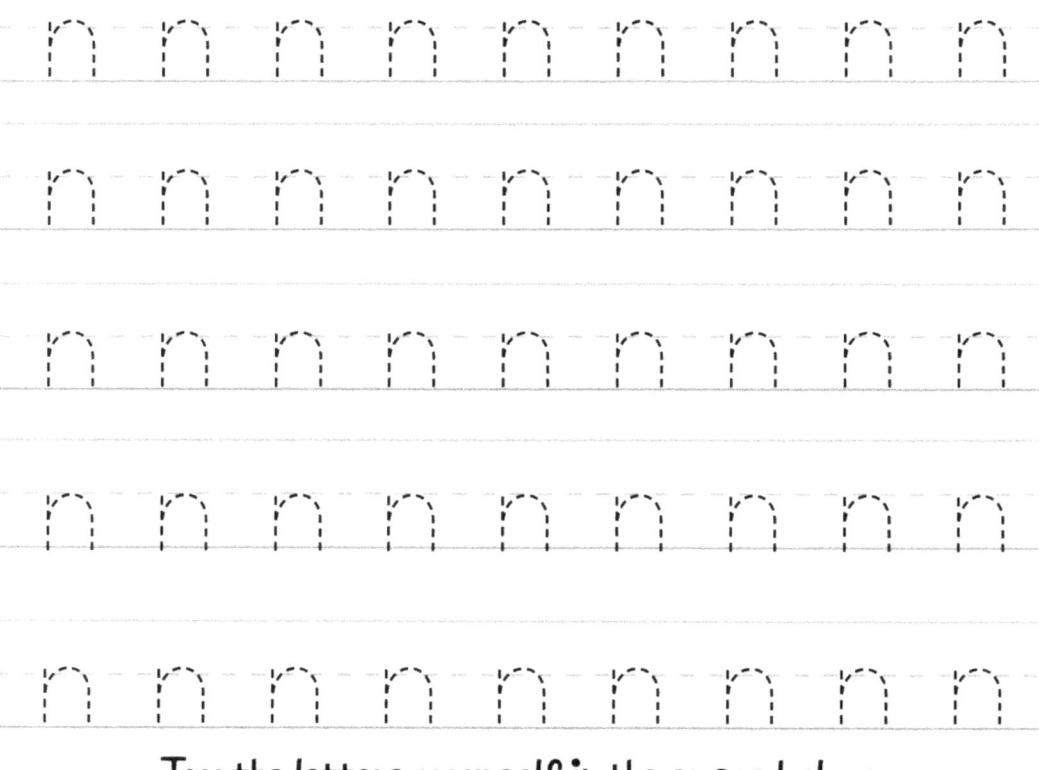

Try the letters yourself in the space below

LETTER

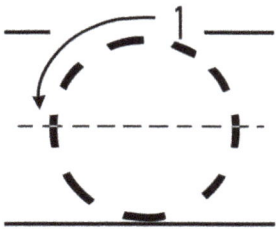

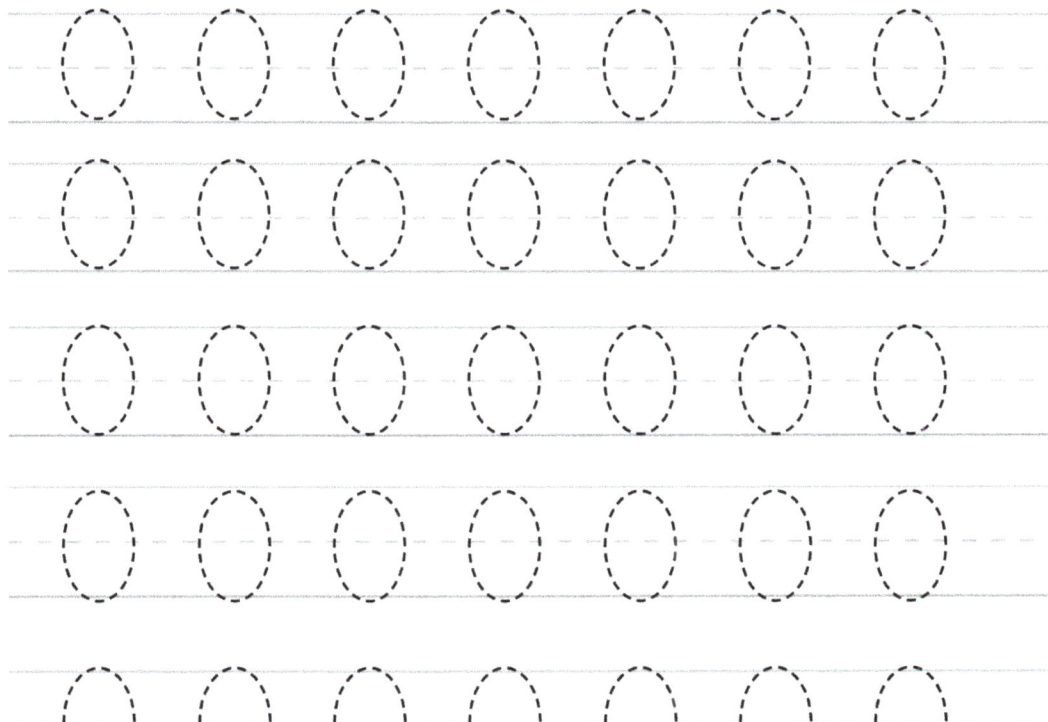

Try the letters yourself in the space below

LETTER

octopus

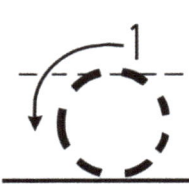

o o o o o o o o o

o o o o o o o o o

o o o o o o o o o

o o o o o o o o o

o o o o o o o o o

Try the letters yourself in the space below

LETTER

Pig

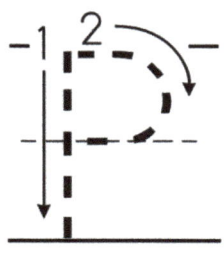

P P P P P P P

P P P P P P P

P P P P P P P

P P P P P P P

P P P P P P P

Try the letters yourself in the space below

LETTER

pencil

Try the letters yourself in the space below

LETTER

 **Q**ueen

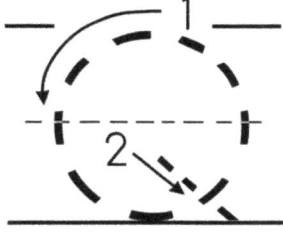

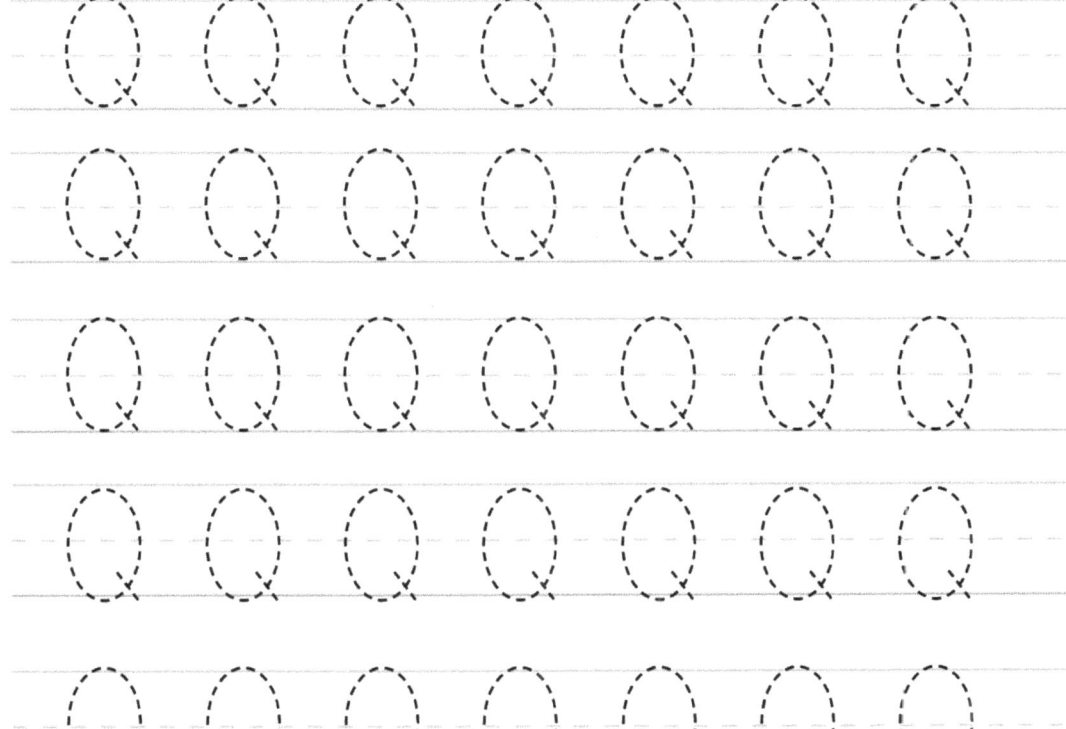

Try the letters yourself in the space below

LETTER

 **q**uiet

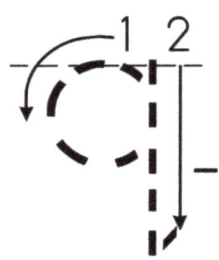

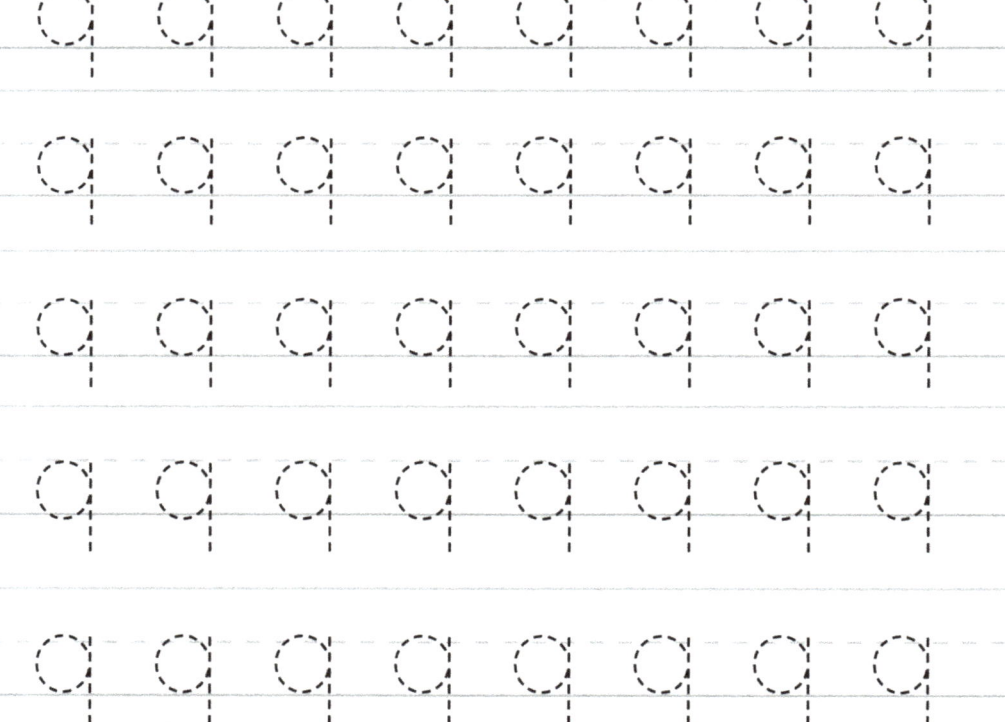

Try the letters yourself in the space below

LETTER

Rooster

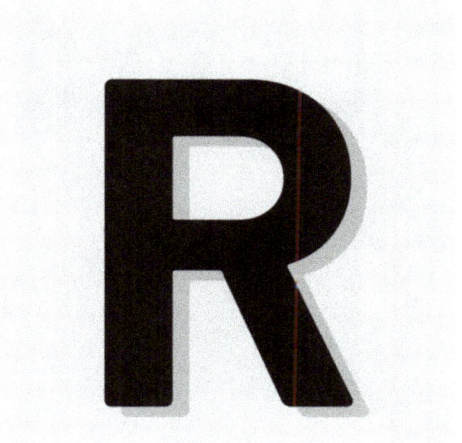

Try the letters yourself in the space below

LETTER

 **r**ope

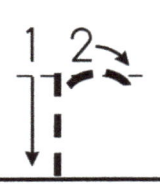

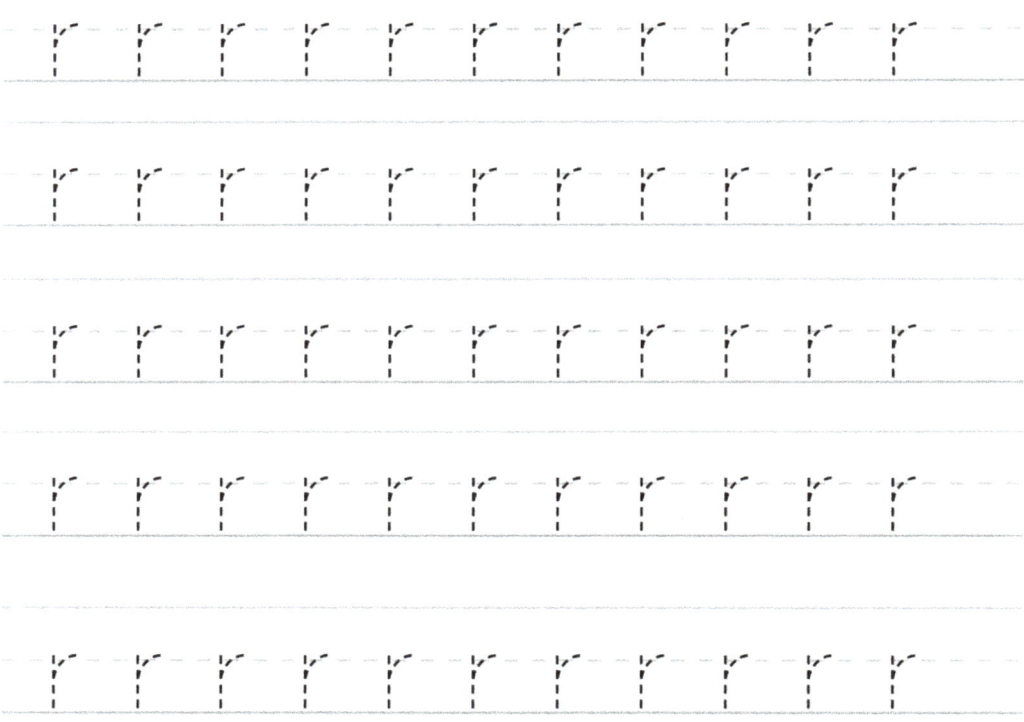

Try the letters yourself in the space below

LETTER

 **S**hip

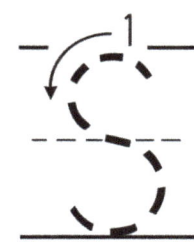

Try the letters yourself in the space below

LETTER

scissors

s s s s s s s s s
s s s s s s s s s
s s s s s s s s s
s s s s s s s s s
s s s s s s s s s

Try the letters yourself in the space below

LETTER

Tiger

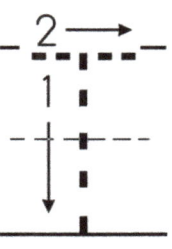

Try the letters yourself in the space below

LETTER

turtle

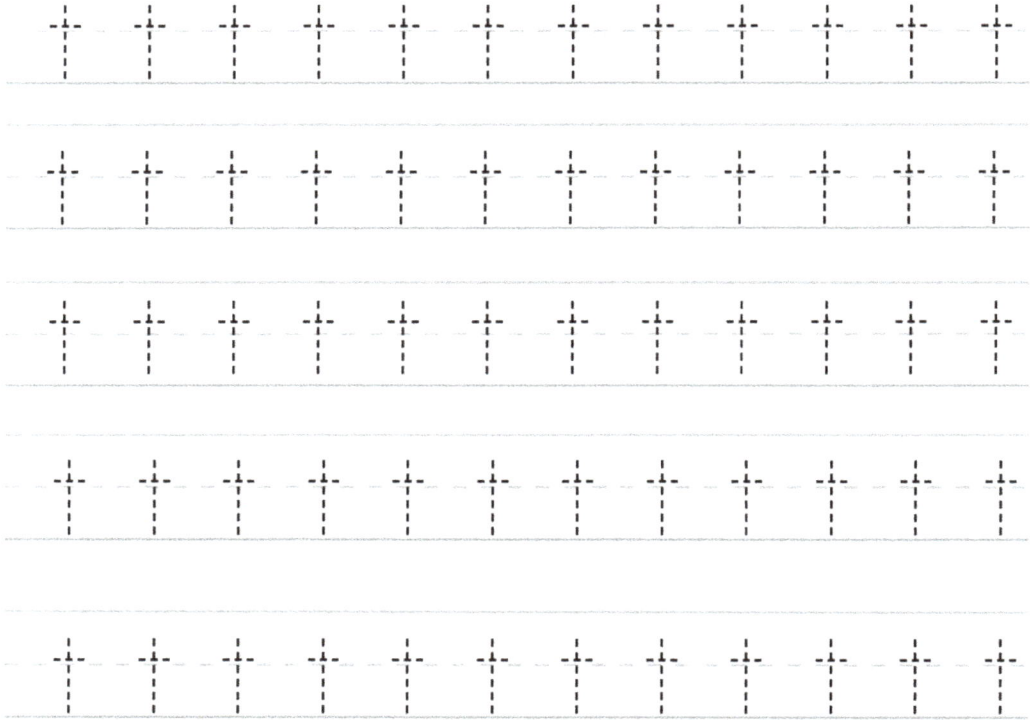

Try the letters yourself in the space below

LETTER

Umbrella

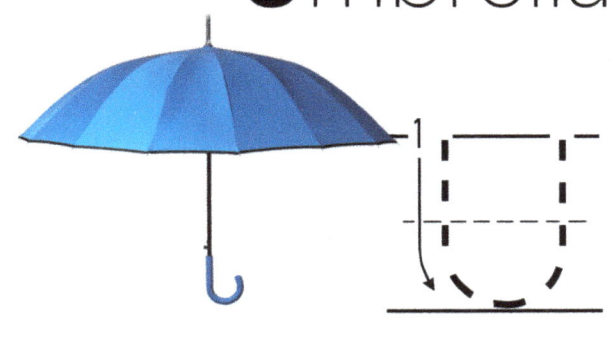

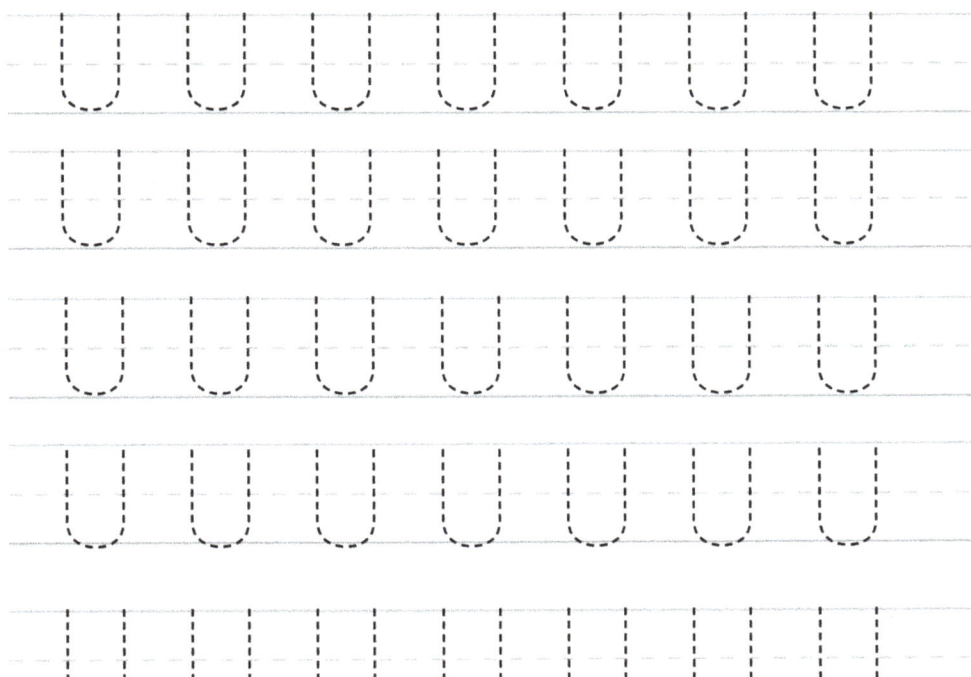

Try the letters yourself in the space below

LETTER

unicycle

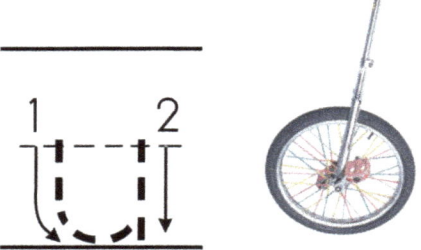

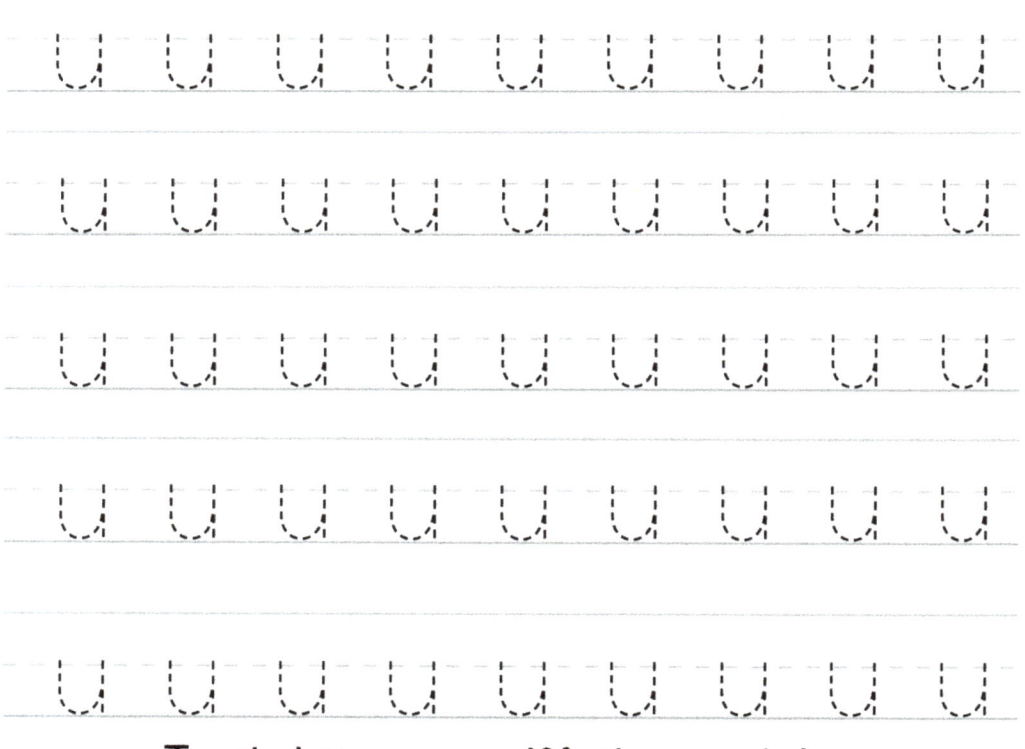

Try the letters yourself in the space below

LETTER

Violin

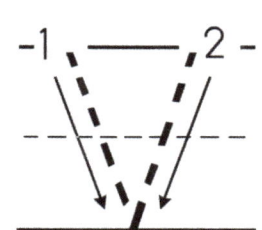
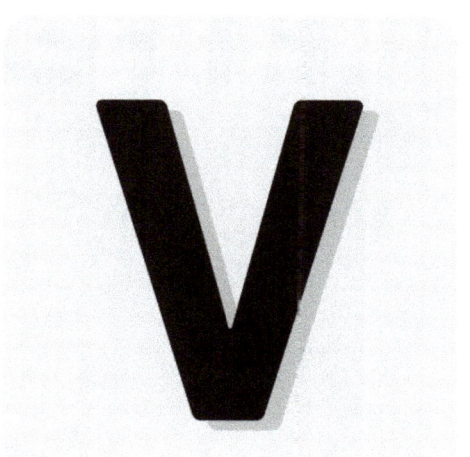

Try the letters yourself in the space below

LETTER V

volcano

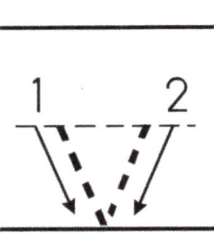  

v v v v v v v v v v

v v v v v v v v v v

v v v v v v v v v v

v v v v v v v v v v

v v v v v v v v v v

Try the letters yourself in the space below

LETTER

Whale

Try the letters yourself in the space below

LETTER

watermelon

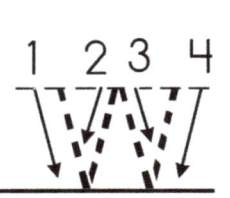

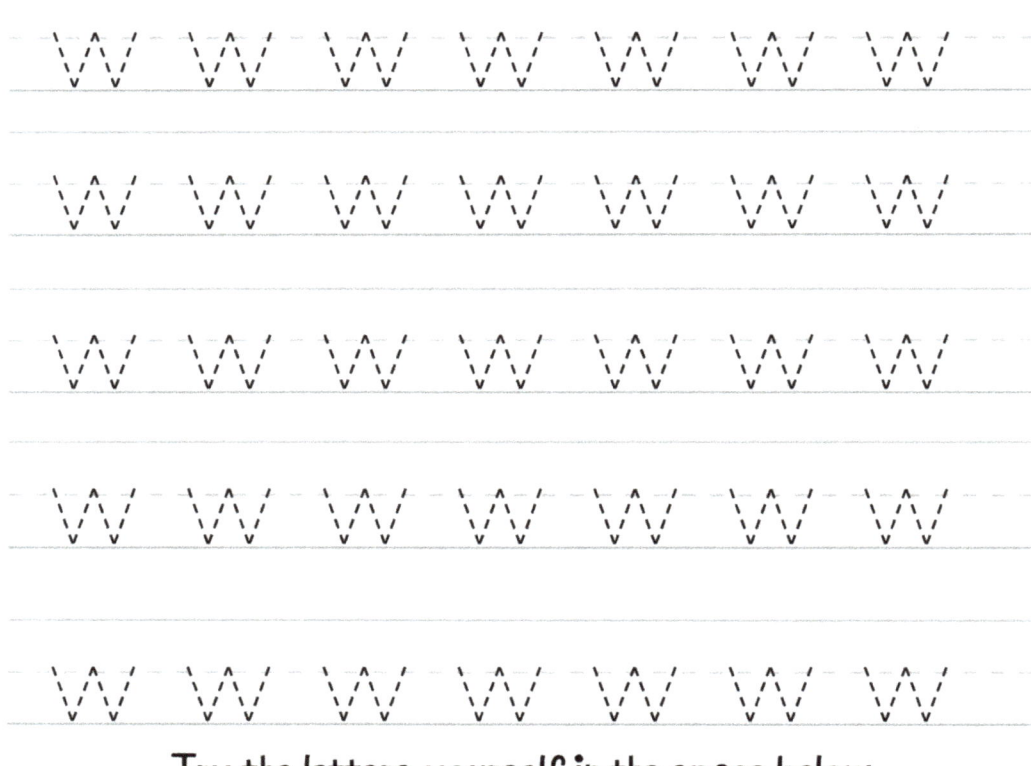

Try the letters yourself in the space below

LETTER

X-ray

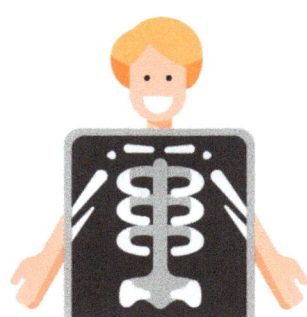
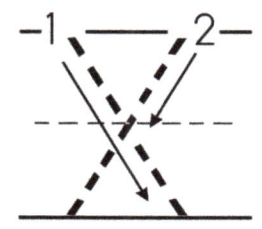

Try the letters yourself in the space below

LETTER

xylophone

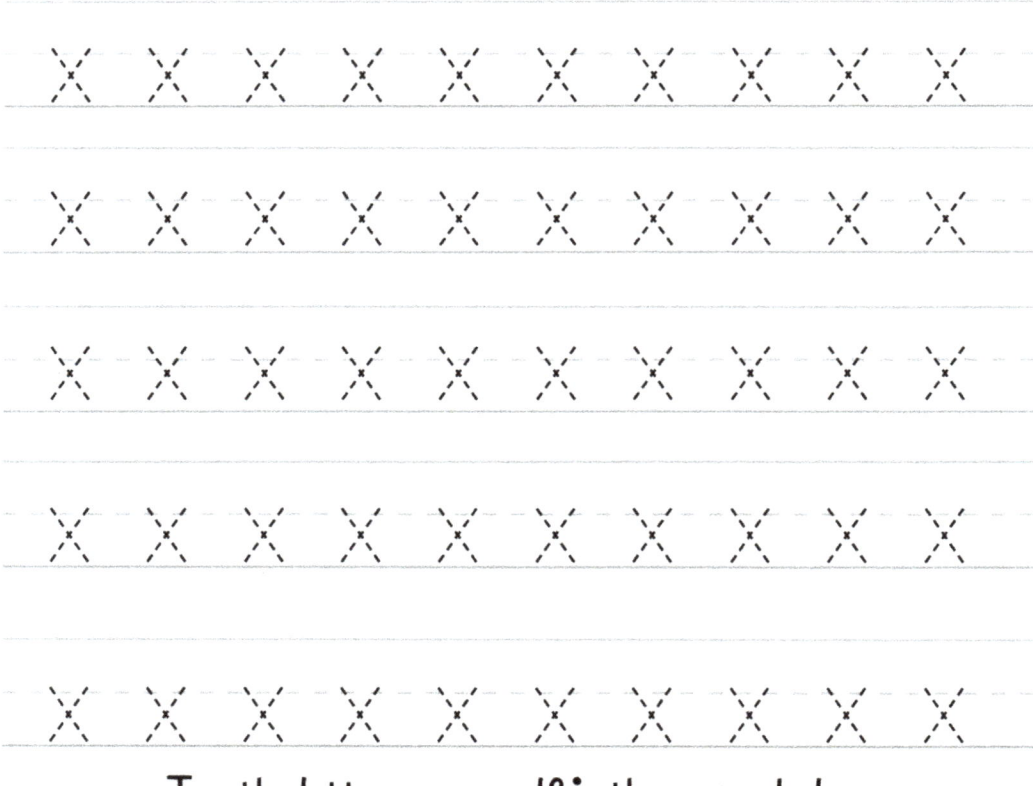

Try the letters yourself in the space below

LETTER

Yolk

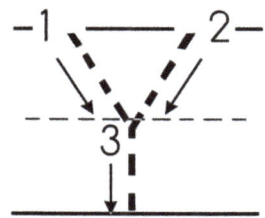

Try the letters yourself in the space below

LETTER

yawn

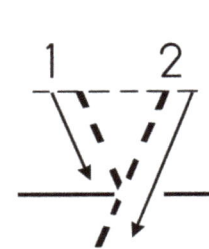

y y y y y y y y y y

y y y y y y y y y y

y y y y y y y y y y

y y y y y y y y y y

y y y y y y y y y y

Try the letters yourself in the space below

LETTER Z

Zoo

Try the letters yourself in the space below

LETTER

zebra

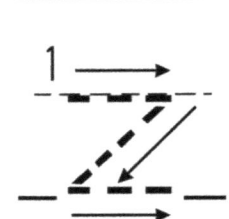

Z

z z z z z z z z z
z z z z z z z z z
z z z z z z z z z
z z z z z z z z z
z z z z z z z z z

Try the letters yourself in the space below

NAME: _____

shadow matching

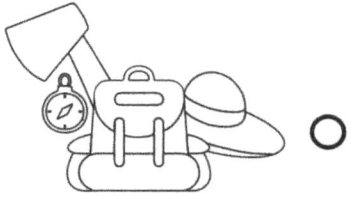 ○   •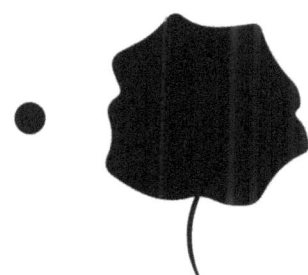

 ○   •

 ○   •

 ○   •

NAME: _____

HELP THE GIRL GET TO THE CAMP

NAME: _____

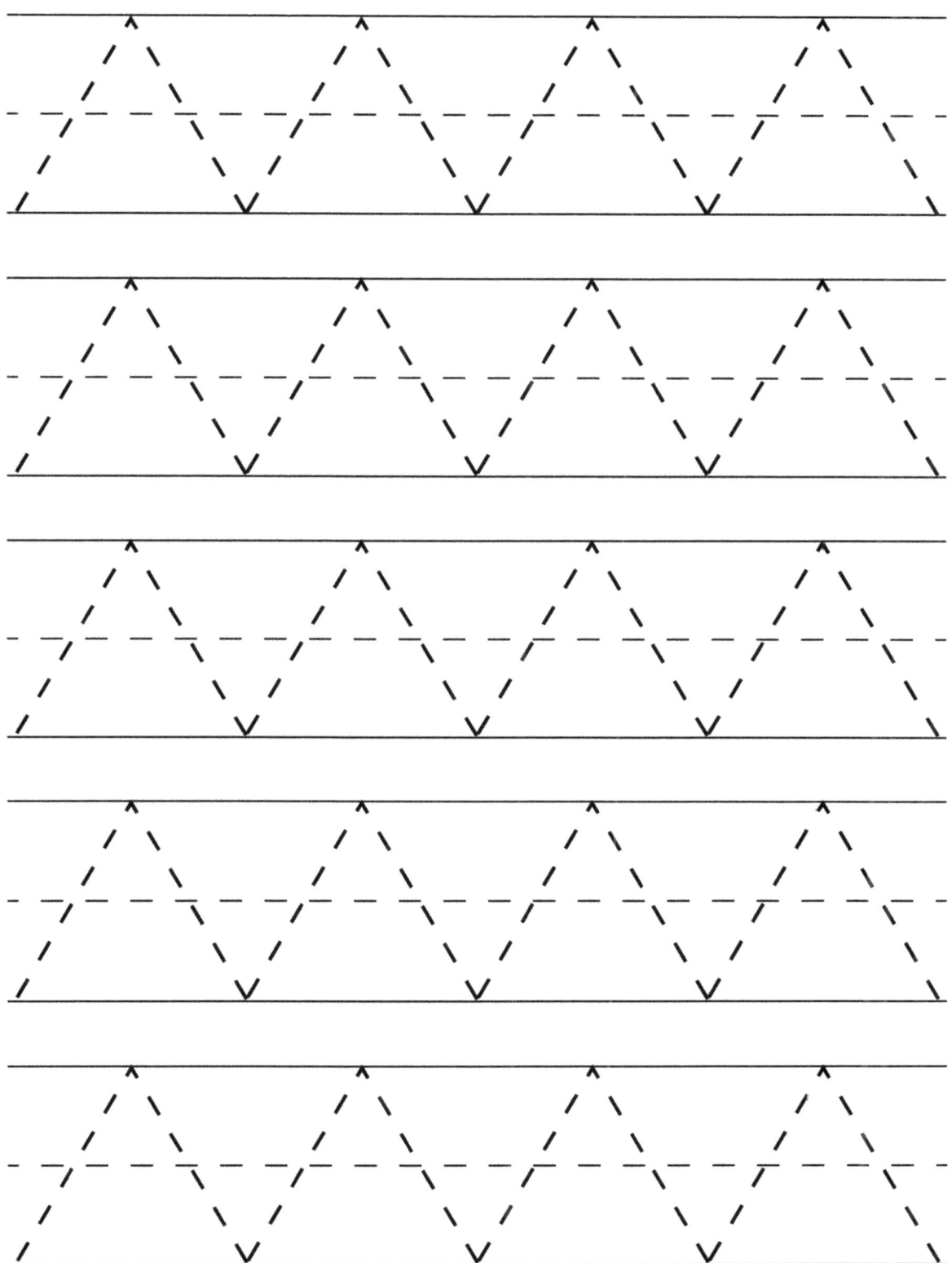

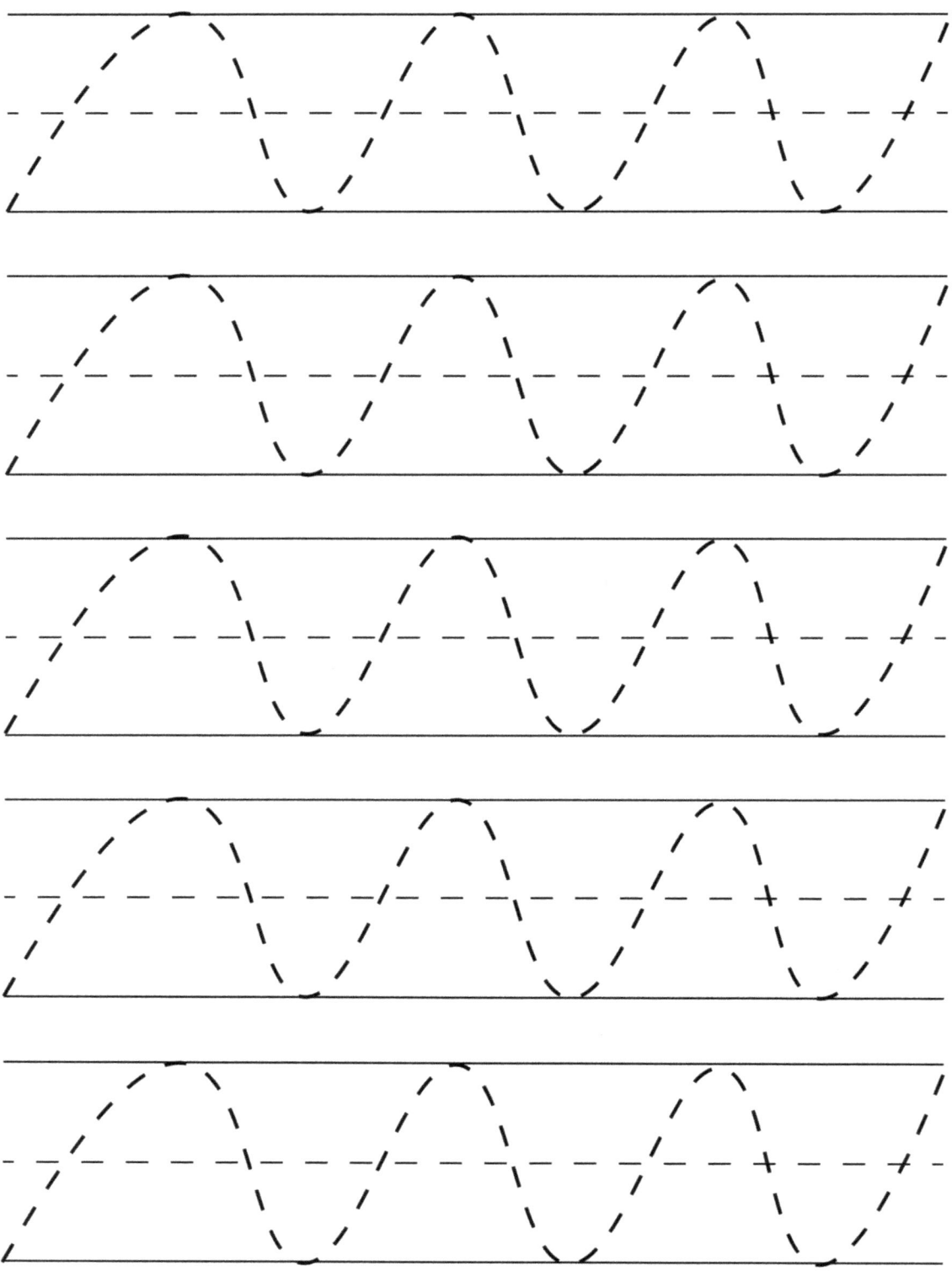

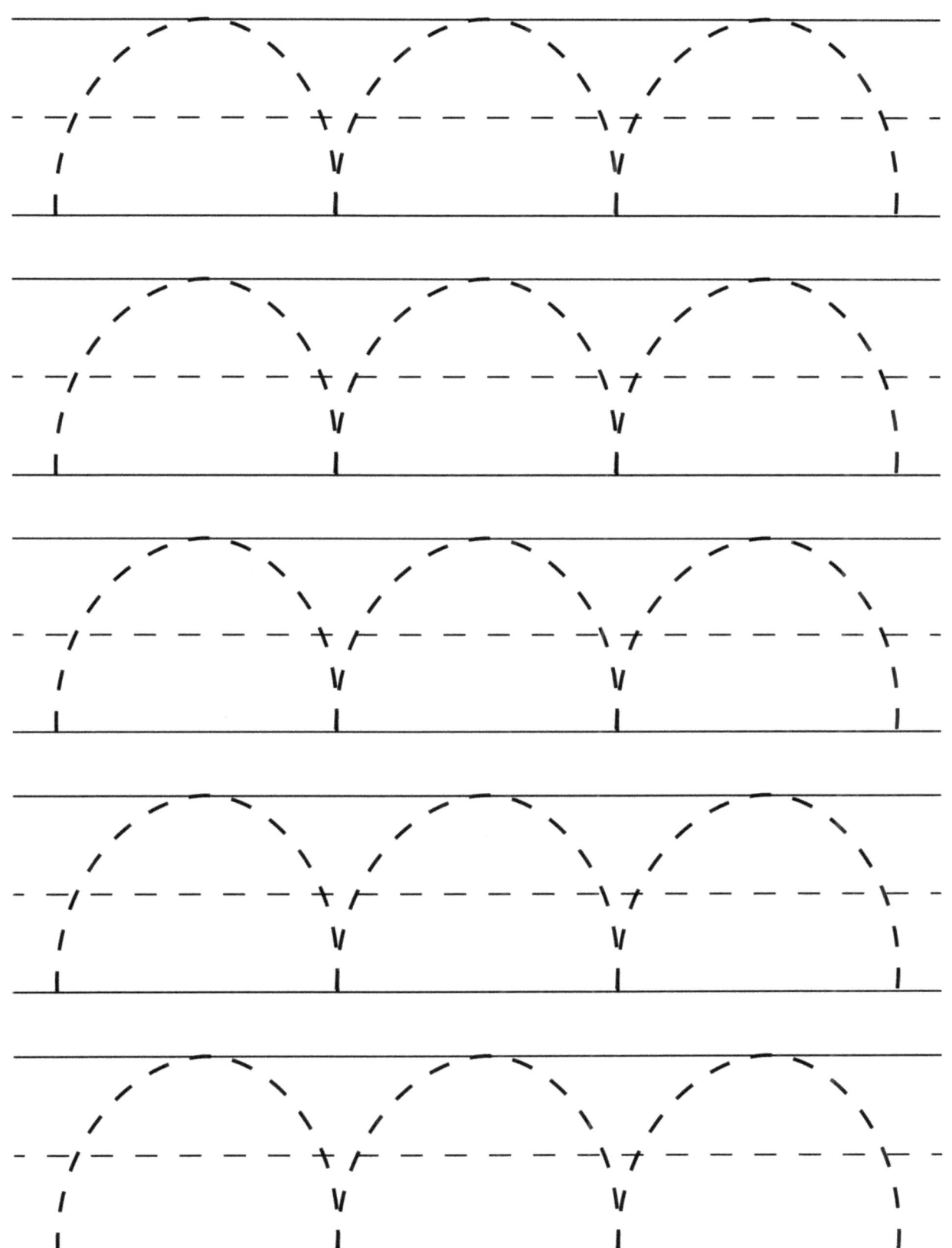

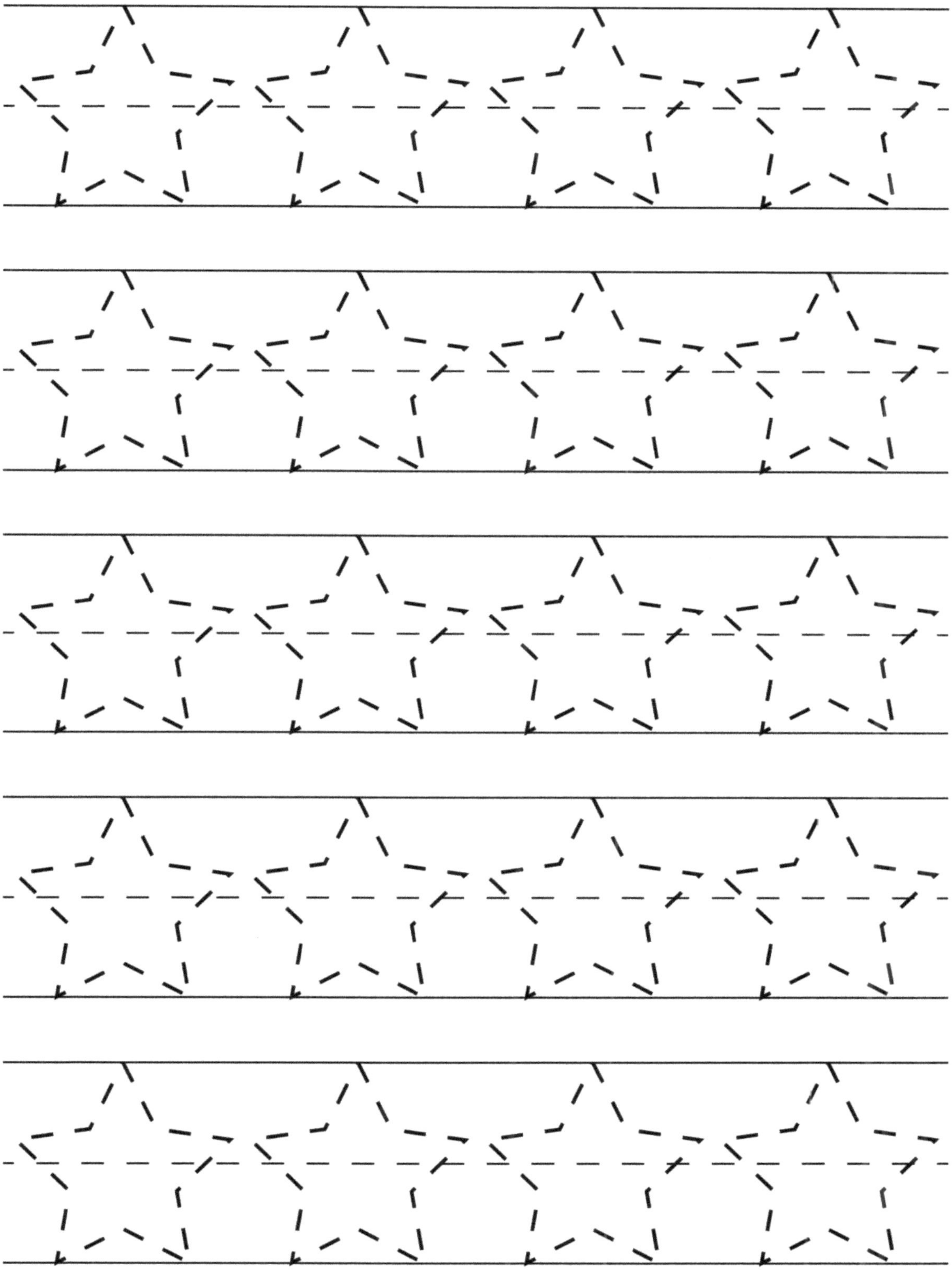

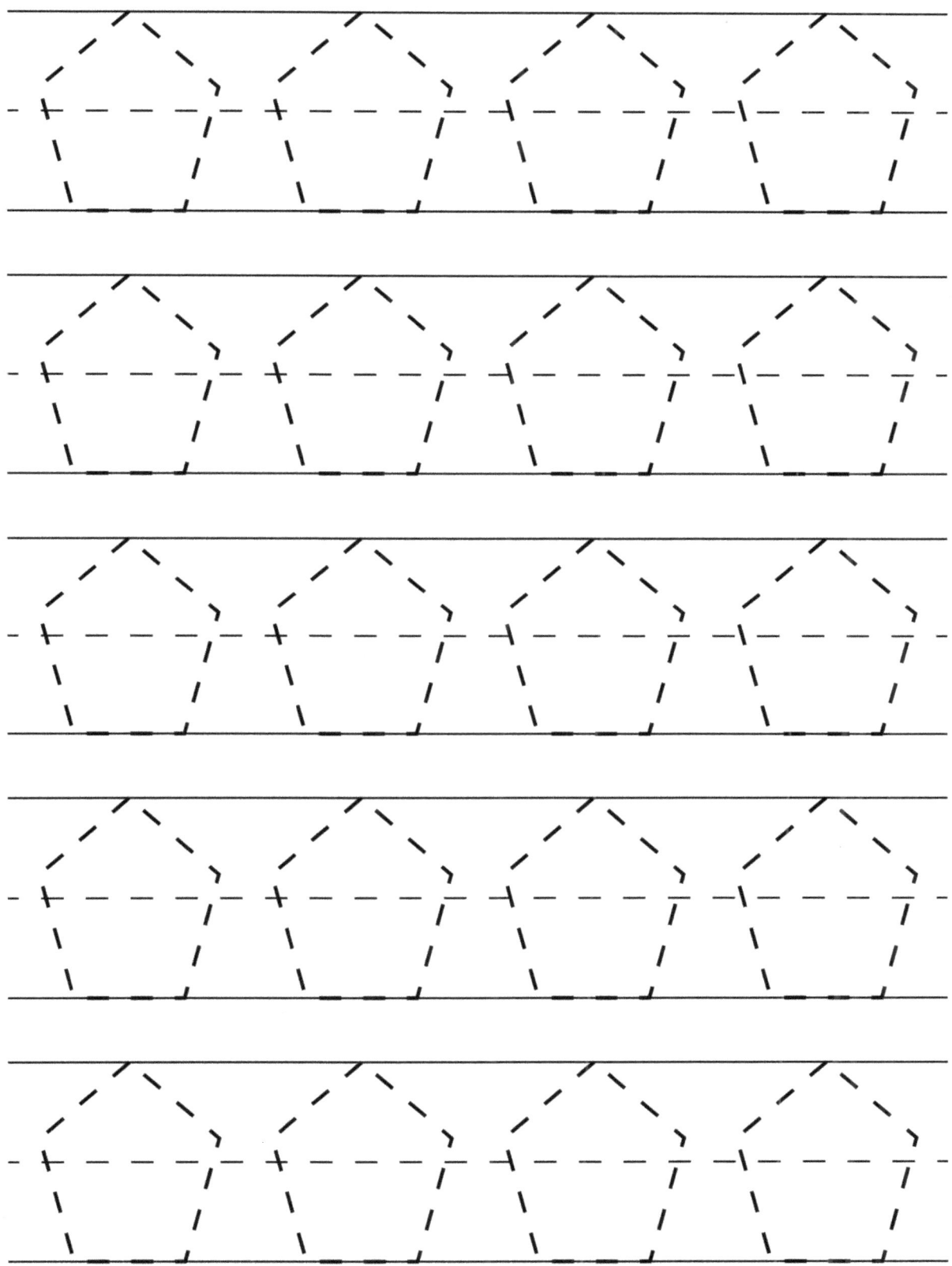

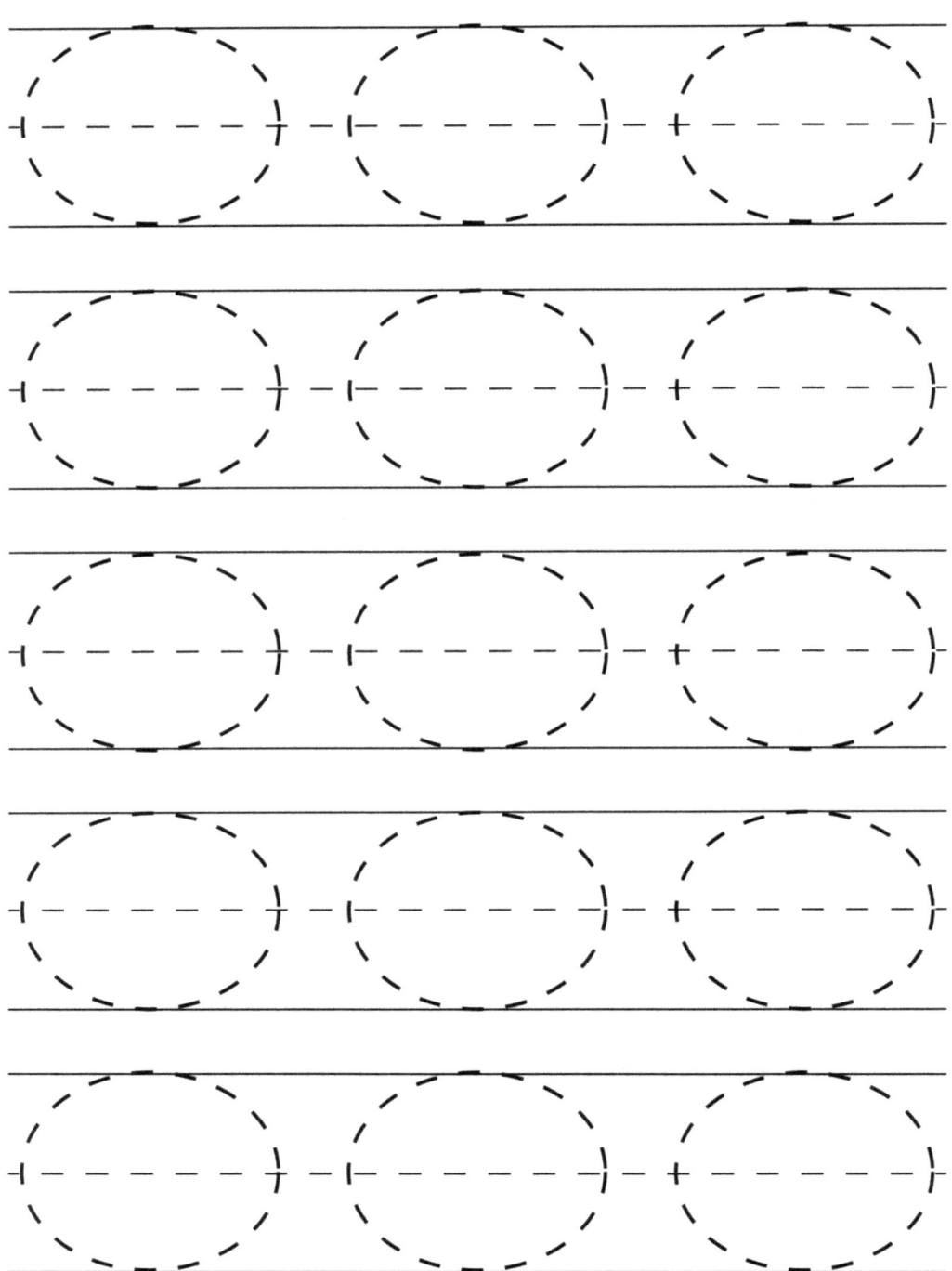